DRAMA QUEEN

by Ginnie Bale

DRAMA QUEEN

Independently Published

ISBN: 978-3-9824152-0-8

Editor: Brooke Goodwin
Instagram: @thewritebrooke

Cover Artwork: Sarah Matsuda
www.sarahmatsuda.com
Instagram: @sarah.matsuda

Cover Design: Ginnie Bale

Ginnie Bale
c/o AutorenServices.de
Birkenallee 24
36037 Fulda

It is not the storm itself I fear,
it is the silence that follows,
the aftermath,
when you slowly realize
you survived
despite the odds,
and there's nothing left
of your old life.

After survival is reconstruction.

to those who love too much
to those who understand
to those who still heal

to the drama queens
who feel

CONTENTS

ACT I:

ONCE UPON A FUCKING TIME

Love is like a sword.

If you don't know how to wield it, it will hurt you.

Loving you is draining me.

No matter how much love I pour into you,
you seem to be bottomless,
desperately craving more.

My dreams turned into nightmares,

the castle into a dungeon,

and the prince, well,

he has always been a dragon,

it just took me much longer to realize it.

I've never felt privileged enough to
reject a feast when one was offered to me.
I've known the bitterness of
deprivation and I was
hungry for love.

Although loving you was
like a permanent starvation.
You fed me just enough to
keep me alive but never enough
to fully satisfy my
craving.

You give me butterflies and self-doubts.

Sometimes I think I'm trying too hard.

That loving you shouldn't take

this much effort.

I was your *pretty little doll*,
dead inside but, oh,
how gorgeous I looked
in those dresses.

Love didn't find me.
It haunted me,
wrestled me to the ground,
wrapped hands around my neck
and squeezed as it gently
kissed my cheek.

The only addiction
I ever suffered was you.
Mistaking it for love,
because neither of us knew
how love was supposed to feel.

Your love was just another bullet
in a war against myself
that I've been fighting
my whole life.

Words don't kill people.

They may wound them,
slowly strangle them,
but never leave
visible marks.

I wish they would.
I wish people could see
how much their
words hurt.

Love is supposed to give you wings,

not rip them from your back.

I held you like an umbrella
until I realized you were
the storm.

Burn me. I will rise from the ashes.

Break me. I will recollect my pieces.

Hurt me. I will heal my wounds.

Drown me. I will learn to breathe under water.

Love me and I will gladly die for you.

He said;

dreams are not reality,

but what he really meant was

my dreams never were

his reality.

You made me feel
like I'm too little
and too much
all at once.

I was your whore,

trading sex for love and affection,

and you paid in small bills.

He loved my brokenness
more than he loved me.

Maybe that's why he
never wanted me to heal.

He stole tiny pieces of me,
unnoticed.

A little bit of confidence,
parts of my intuition,
fragments of happiness.

Then he replaced them
with pieces of himself:
doubts,
insecurity,
fear.

He never liked his woman strong.
He couldn't control
her that way.

We tasted every flavor of love –

from sweet to bitter.

Love is a loaded gun,
but it was you who
aimed at my heart and
pulled the trigger.

I said, 'you've changed'.

You laughed and called me silly.

I always trusted you more than myself.

He painted me in black and white,
but I never considered
he might be
colorblind.

You didn't want me,
but you couldn't stand the thought
someone else might
have me.

That's not love.

We only called it love
because possession is an ugly word.

He didn't like drama

and I was fucking Shakespeare.

I wonder if
you were
the poison
or the antidote?

"Why do you love me?" he asked.

"Because I don't know how to stop."

What's the point of staying,

when loving you and leaving hurts the same?

ACT II:

A KINGDOM OF PAIN

Falling feels like flying until
you hit the ground.

My heart is a crime scene without a suspect.

Too many wounds and bruises to tell

which ones you caused,

and if this heartbreak killed me,

or if I died a long time ago.

Loving you was so convenient,
at least I didn't need to hurt myself anymore.

Maybe it was naïve to believe
you would catch me when I fall,
when it was always you
who pushed me.

How am I supposed to cut you off without hurting
myself, when I don't know where you end
and I begin?

You broke so much more than just my heart.

I loved you even when I hated you.

Maybe this tore my heart apart
more than your betrayal.

Perhaps we used each other to prove
we were capable of feeling more
than just pain.

How am I supposed to let go
when holding on is the only thing
that keeps me from
falling apart?

"But why did you stay?"

"Because he silenced my noise like no other drug."

Pain is my lover,

it fucks me hard but

never stays to hold me when I cry.

I wish I could tell you how much you hurt me,
but I fear you might use my vulnerability
to hurt me even more.

My masochistic heart longs for
your torment.

(*I'm just trying to say I miss you.*)

The door was always open for you to leave,
you didn't need to burn the house down
to get out.

I'm not lost.
I'm hiding,

in places where pain
can't find me.

The pain you caused, I framed it,
hung it on a wall next to childhood memories,
revisiting it from time to time,
only to wonder why it still hurts.

Memories don't fade unless you burn them.

Sometimes we need to cry to wash away the dirt from our souls.

You don't blame a knife
for cutting, do you?

Why do we blame love for
the pain we feel?

But I can't love a heart that nurtures
itself with tears.

Eventually, I listened to the pain.

"Let go", it whispered.

ACT III:

FAIRY TALES OF LIES

Love is not good or bad,

it is every emotion in between.

I'm stuck somewhere between wanting you
and the desire to feel free.

We both lied.

You lied when you said you
don't want to change me,
and I lied when I said I
wouldn't let you.

Why is it so hard to stop loving you when
it seems so easy for you
to hurt me?

Waiting for closure is just another excuse I tell
myself because I'm not ready to
let go.

He taught me that
I love you doesn't mean *I won't hurt you,*
I love you doesn't mean *I am here for you,*
I love you doesn't mean *I keep you safe.*

And now I'm afraid to hear those words.

Hope is cruel.

I told her leaving was the right thing to do,
and she whispered,

"Was it?"

I'm used to people hurting me.
I just didn't think you'd be
one of them.

If only you had realized that I didn't
build those walls to shut you out,
but to protect my heart.

Maybe you might have been
more gentle when
you tore them down.

I didn't know how to love you
and love myself at the same time.
You always made
me choose.

And I always chose you.

Some day you might realize how toxic you were,
but I won't be there to say
I told you so.

I was afraid of losing you
when I should have been more afraid of
losing myself in you.

What a shame,

that you discovered every inch of my body,

and not the slightest piece

of my *soul*.

I will always remember
these two things about you:

What you did *for* me
and
what you did *to* me.

If I could turn back time,
I'd love you a little less
and love myself
a little more instead.

The more I miss you,

the more I come up with excuses

why it wasn't that bad, what you did,

but I always end up with

the same realization:

it was.

— *lies I keep telling myself*

Loving you was more of an addiction I suffered;
the kind you barely survive.

My heart may be broken,

but it is still beating,

every beat a declaration of war,

never surrendering to the pain

you caused.

The way we hurt each other reflects
how others have hurt us.

When I left, I thought my world would end.

But it just stopped for a moment,
starting again to spin
only slower,
gentler,
almost
peacefully.

I will hold your memory in a special place,
locked behind bars where it can't
hurt me anymore.

It's ironic that you were once
the reason I believed in love,
and now you are every reason
I fear it.

I burned every bridge that led to you,
neglecting that I've walked
through fire for you
before.

Don't give up on love.

Give up on the person who was not able to
love you *the way you deserve*.

I wonder if you would have loved me differently
if someone had taught you
how to love yourself.

I wonder if I would have left earlier
if someone had taught me
how to love myself.

You destroyed me, thinking I'd beg you to fix me.
You didn't expect me to fix myself, did you?

(You never believed in me anyway.)

I wish my heart would stop grieving over you.
You don't deserve any of
my emotions.

You said no one will love me the way you did,
and I hope you're right.

I don't hate you.

I only hate the parts of you
that destroyed me.

Sometimes I wish I was still the person
I was before you broke me.
The old me.

But then I'd still be
a woman who stays with a man
that makes her feel less than herself,
and I don't want to be that
woman anymore.

I'm not.

I still hear your voice,

whispering that I'm not good enough,

but I finally decided not to

listen anymore.

Trust is like a crystal vase.
Once it breaks, it shatters.

You can recollect most of the pieces,
but some will always remain missing.
And, even if you put it back
together again,

it will never be the same.

I believed you wouldn't hurt me
and you believed I would never leave.

Guess we were both wrong.

Because you were the reason

I believed in love.

Because you were there

when no one else was.

Because you stayed

when everyone walked away.

Because you promised you'd never leave,

and I thought that was a good thing.

Because you said you wouldn't change,

and I believed you.

— reasons I stayed (when I should have left)

Your poison still runs through my veins,
but it is not strong enough to
affect my heart anymore.

You were my favorite comfort sweater,
the one stretched out and faded
from wearing it too much,
until one day you didn't
seem to fit anymore.

You pulled too tightly on my body
and left my skin itchy.

Sometimes love is not a promise,
but a threat to your happiness.

My only revenge is that I will worship
the parts of me you refused to
love.

ACT IV:

THE QUEEN AND HER
GLASS SLIPPERS

Happiness is as fragile as my heart.

I used to dream of being a princess, and maybe I am.

Except my slippers are made of broken glass and the prince choked me instead of chasing me.

— *fucked up fairy tale*

It's not that I don't want to love myself,
it's just that I don't know
how to.

I am deep waters,

afraid to drown in my depths.

I loved you exactly the way I am,

messy and wild,
and a little too much.

I don't know how to be vulnerable.

I only know how to be strong,
even when I'm breaking.

This is me. This is how I am.

I will always hope, always love,

and always break

because

of it.

I won't hide my scars any longer
just because they don't match
your beauty standards.

I only drowned
because all that time I
was waiting for someone
to save me.

I didn't believe
I could
swim.

I'm too stubborn to remain broken.
I would never give you
so much power
over me.

Love is not a game of chess.

The queen doesn't sacrifice herself
for the king.

If you think of me,

I want you to remember

that I am the storm

you could not tame.

I'm sorry I am not the woman
you wanted me to be.

I'm sorry
I am so much more.

No one saw her suffer.

She made walking through fire look beautiful,
as if she danced with the flames.

If it wasn't for your sharp edges,
you'd still be held hostage in a life
that wasn't meant for you.

You freed yourself
from the chains that held you
captive for so long.

I realized I am not a princess,
I am the castle.

Walls of stone,
almost impossible to conquer,
a fortress built to protect hidden treasures,
weapons ready to fight any enemy.

I'm not a princess,
and I don't need saving.
I've always saved myself.

There's this longing in my heart,
whispering,

"I wish someone would stay."

Those walls I built to protect my heart,
they don't leave much space
for visitors.

Some days I am steel,
some days the fire that forged it,
and some days I am the
wind which fuels that fire.

You say I'm fragile as if there's something
wrong with that.

The most precious things are fragile,
and only those who know their value will
protect them and keep them safe.

Don't put your heart on sale
because of its bruises.

In time, you will find someone
who treasures your vintage heart
like the one of a kind art it is.

You said I'm nothing without you.

Now let me show you how
much you're wrong.

ACT V:

THE ~~ENDING~~ BEGINNING

Loving you was tiring.

Leaving you was *liberating*.

Growth comes after destruction.

After wildfires,
storms,
you.

I didn't survive the storm to drown
in the aftermath.

I'm not giving up,
I just give my wings time to rest.

And I swear I will heal

from the wounds you caused,

for I promised myself I won't keep

any memories of you.

The strong ones are not those who never break.

They are the ones that refuse
to stay broken.

Maybe time will
heal my wounds,
but even if time doesn't,
I will.

I sacrificed my heart for you.

I won't do the same with my happiness.

You cut my heart in pieces and hope grew
from the wounds.

— *how I learned to survive*

I learned to follow my intuition,

because my heart

only leads me

back to you.

It is comforting to know that one can break
and heal at the same time. I am hurting,
but I welcome the pain of growth.

In fact, I embrace it.

It is okay that today is not
the day you are ready to let go.
Some day you will.

— *there's always tomorrow*

And if you must hold onto something,
why don't you hold on to yourself
and let go of the love that only
hurts you?

One day I will shine, just not in your sky.

I grow happiness around the
sadness that lives inside of me,
like flowers on a battlefield.

This year I learned that even if there are
empty spaces in my heart,
I don't have to
let anyone in.

You have to earn
your place.

I thought I needed to get stronger
to carry the weight on my shoulders,
when all I needed to do was
to let it go.

I exhale you.

What's the point of holding on
to something that doesn't
nurture me?

Letting go of you is so much easier
than letting go of the pain
you caused.

I love the rain.
It reminds me that new beginnings
don't necessarily have to be
bright and shiny.

Day 158:
I thought about you
and didn't cry.

Is this how healing is
supposed to feel?

Forgiveness doesn't have to be earned.

Sometimes it is a gift to ourselves
to release the heaviness
from our hearts.

You used to be a wound in my chest
that wouldn't stop bleeding.

Now you're only scar tissue,
a reminder that I can heal
from anything.

This remains a love story.

I just replaced your name with my own.

— *(self) love story*

Stop invalidating your feelings
just because others do.

Embrace every emotion,
feel whatever you feel,
grow from it.

Go on a date with yourself.

Buy flowers.

Eat as much ice cream as you want

and don't feel guilty about it.

Treat yourself the way

you treat others.

Love yourself the way

you love others.

Maybe loving myself
will come naturally one day.

Until then, I will keep
fighting for it.

I hope I never forget you.

I want to remember the pain.

I want to celebrate the

victory over it.

ACKNOLEDGEMENT

I don't even know where to begin to express my gratitude for the love and support I receive from the people in my life.

I'm grateful for the huge number of people I was lucky enough to meet on Instagram over the last year. Thank you for your support and for believing in me, even when I sometimes forget to believe in myself.

There are too many names to mention, just know that you fill my heart with love and make it so easy to open up and be vulnerable and share my deepest thoughts and fears with you.

I'm forever grateful for the support and love of the poetry community and the friends I found there. You inspire me every day to become a better writer and the best version of myself.

Thank you to Sarah Matsuda, the incredibly talented Australian artist who painted the artwork for my book cover. I couldn't have asked for a better artist to bring my idea to life.

Thank you to Brooke Goodwin for editing my book baby. I loved working with you so much.

Thank you to André, for being there when no one else was (and is). Thank you for reading my books, even if you don't like poetry — or feelings at all. Thank you for being the best friend I could ask for.

Thank you to my beautiful sister, for your never-ending support on every step of my book writing journey and in life.

Thank you to Charly, for being my first "fan" or at least the first person I shared my poems with, tipsy on champagne on my 30th birthday, at a roof-top bar in Paris. Paris is not only for lovers, but also for friends.

ABOUT THE AUTHOR

Ginnie Bale is a German writer and poet.

After experiencing several traumatic events in her life, Ginnie discovered the healing power of reading and writing poetry.

She holds a Master of Arts in Management and Media and wanted to become a journalist for most of her life, until she found her purpose in writing poetry and fiction and helping people through sharing her experiences.

With her writing, Ginnie hopes to inspire people, be a voice for the voiceless and a light to those who need it.

Ginnie is a mental health advocate and feminist who writes about love, self-love, trauma and healing.

If you would like to support the author and her work, please consider leaving a brief review on Amazon or Goodreads, or send her a DM.

E-Mail: ginniebalepoetry@gmail.com

Follow Ginnie Bale on social media:

Instagram: @ginniebalepoetry
TikTok: @ginniebale
Facebook: Ginnie Bale

Printed in Great Britain
by Amazon

86709508R00090